AF673173

My First Book of
Little Devis

This Book Belongs To

____

Ma Durga

Little Devi, Little Devi,
Ma Durga!
Riding a tiger,
Will you bless me?

Little one, little one,
Yes, my little one!
I'll make you so brave,
You just have fun!

DID YOU KNOW?

Ma Durga turned the asuras into ashes by just saying "HMMM"

Mahalakshmi

Little Devi, Little Devi,
Mahalakshmi!
Sitting on a lotus,
Will you bless me?

Little one, little one,
Yes, my little one!
I'll take care of all your needs,
You just have fun!

DID YOU KNOW?

Mahalakshmi has 8 forms known as Ashtalakshmi. She blesses us with 8 types of wealth.

Saraswati

Little Devi, Little Devi,
Saraswati!
Holding a veena,
Will you bless me?

Little one, little one,
Yes, my little one!
I'll help you learn everything,
You just have fun!

DID YOU KNOW?

Saraṣwati holds a veena, a book and a japamala in her hands.

Kamakshi

Little Devi, Little Devi,
Kamakshi!
With eyes so pretty,
Will you bless me?

Little one, little one,
Yes, my little one!
I'll grant all your wishes,
You just have fun!

DID YOU KNOW?

Kamakshi holds a sugarcane, parrot and a bunch of flowers in her hands.

Meenakshi

Little Devi, Little Devi,
Meenakshi!
With eyes like a fish,
Will you bless me?

Little one, little one,
Yes, my little one!
I'll watch over you,
You just have fun!

DID YOU KNOW?

Just as the fish never closes its eyes, Meenakshi is always watching over us.

Vishalakshi

Little Devi, Little Devi,
Vishalakshi!
With such a broad vision,
Will you bless me?

Little one, little one,
Yes, my little one!
I'll make you kind and caring,
You just have fun!

DID YOU KNOW?

Vishalakshi holds a Shivling, Ganesha, Kamandala and Japamala and her vahana is the deer.

Bhuvaneshvari

Little Devi, Little Devi,
Bhuvaneshvari!
Mother of the universe,
Will you bless me?

Little one, little one,
Yes, my little one!
I'll make the whole world
your friend,
You just have fun!

DID YOU KNOW?

Bhuvaneshvari is the queen mother of the whole universe!

Annapoorni

Little Devi, Little Devi,
Annapoorni!
Holding a bowl of *payasam,
Will you bless me?

Little one, little one,
Yes, my little one!
I'll make you happy and sweet,
You just have fun!

DID YOU KNOW?

Annapoorni has generous pots of treats and desserts for all.

*Sweet porridge.

Balambika

Little Devi, Little Devi,
Balambika!
So young and sweet,
Will you bless me?

Little one, little one,
Yes, my little one!
I'll protect your innocence,
You just have fun!

DID YOU KNOW?

Balambika is the child goddess. She is full of innocence and enthusiasm.

Parashakti

Little Devi, Little Devi,
Parashakti!
Shining as a brilliant light,
Will you bless me?

Little one, little one,
Yes, my little one!
I'll make you powerful,
You just have fun!

DID YOU KNOW?

All the devis are a part of Parashakti!

Little Devis, Little Devis,
Jagat Janani!
I want the whole world to be happy,
Will you bless me?

Sarvamangala mangalye
Shive sarvaartha sadhike
Sharanye tryambake Gauri
Narayani namostute

सर्वमंगलमांगल्ये शिवे सर्वार्थसाधिके ।
शरण्ये त्र्यम्बके गौरी नारायणि नमोऽस्तु ते ॥

Sharanaagata deenaartha
paritraana paraayane
Sarvasyarti hare devi
naaraayani namostute

शरणागत दीनार्थ परित्राण परायणे
सर्वस्यार्तिहरे देवि नारायणि नमोऽस्तु ते ॥

Little one, Little one,
Yes, my little one!
We are all by your side!
You just have fun!